THE
A B I D E
BIBLE COURSE

*Five Practices to Help You Engage
with God through Scripture*

STUDY GUIDE | SIX SESSIONS

PHIL COLLINS & RANDY FRAZEE
with J.R. Briggs

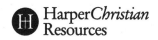

Harper*Christian*
Resources

CONTENTS

INTRODUCTION

People experience the Bible in a wide variety of ways. Some find it to be a wonderful, joy-infused, life-giving experience which guides their lives and draws them closer to God. But for many, reading the Bible can seem intimidating—a big book with lots of hard to pronounce names written thousands of years ago.

Maybe you find it confusing, overwhelming—even daunting—and you wonder where to begin. Or maybe you're convinced that reading the Bible is a good thing, an experience that can give life, which God uses to teach people of all ages.

Maybe you've experienced those moments of ecstasy and joy, where you've heard from the Lord and felt drawn to dig in to God's Word even deeper. And yet, you've found those moments to be few and far between. After being consistent for a few weeks, you stop reading. Eventually you try to muster up the strength to re-engage with it once again.

And maybe, as a result, you struggle with feelings of frustration or disappointment or guilt that you aren't as consistent as you want to be. You want to be more consistent, but you just don't know how.

Rest assured, you're not alone. And rest even more assured this study is not some gimmicky approach or half-hearted attempt to lead you down a path of more stops and starts. This study is intended to be different because the approach to the Bible is entirely different.

The primary goal of reading the Bible isn't to know the Bible; instead, it's to *know the God of the Bible.* You have the opportunity to know God first-hand, just as the writers of Scripture knew God first-hand. This study is intended to be different because the approach to the Bible is entirely different. The goal is not for you to merely read the Bible, but actually to engage with Scripture.

It's common to read the Bible only from the neck up. Reading from the neck up certainly has its benefits, but this study encourages you to also read from the neck down. The best way for you to *experience* God through Scripture is to *engage* with it. And to engage requires a willingness to participate in it. It would be easy to watch the videos in this study, jot down a few notes, discuss a few ideas with others, and go home each week. But this is an invitation for you to participate further and engage deeper.

In this study you'll be encouraged to participate in a variety of practices. Some will feel natural; others might feel different or new. Not all scripture engagement practices will be a perfect fit for everyone. There is no one size fits all. But the encouragement is this: press in anyway. Participate—and then see which practices resonate with you and your Scripture engagement "personality." Pay attention to which ones work and which ones are more difficult—and then lean in farther with where you sense the Lord is meeting you in your time in his Word.

HOW TO USE THIS GUIDE

Structure of the Study

This *Abide Bible Course* is designed to help you experience Scripture with others in a group setting. It may be in a small group or Sunday school class context—or a gathering of friends, co-workers, or neighbors in a living room—physical or digital. If your group or gathering is larger in size, consider breaking off into smaller groupings of five to seven people so that everyone can participate and allow a great opportunity to get the most out of the times together.

Materials Needed

Everyone in your group will need a copy of this study guide, which includes the opening questions to discuss, notes for the video teachings, directions for activities and discussion questions, and personal studies in between sessions. It would be helpful to use a Bible as well. The translation you desire to use is completely up to you. (If you are looking to purchase a Bible, consider *The Abide Bible*. It was created to help you with these Scripture engagement exercises. See the end of this study guide for more information about *The Abide Bible.*)

Facilitation

While everyone will participate in practices together, it is important that your group appoints someone as a facilitator. A facilitator will be responsible for starting the video and keeping track of time during discussions and activities. Facilitators may also read questions aloud and monitor discussions, prompting everyone in the group to respond, and assuring and reminding everyone that each person has the opportunity to participate. If you have been chosen for this role, there are additional instructions and resources available to you in the back of this guide to help you lead your group members through the study.

Personal Studies

During the week, you can maximize the impact of the course with the personal studies provided for each session. You can treat each personal study section like a devotional and use them in whatever way works best for your schedule. You could do one section each day for three days of the week or complete them all in one sitting. These personal studies are not intended to be burdensome or time-consuming, but to provide a richer experience and continuity in between your group sessions.

SESSION ONE

ABIDE IN CHRIST

I am the vine; you are the branches. If you remain in me and I in you, you will bear much fruit; apart from me you can do nothing. If you do not remain in me, you are like a branch that is thrown away and withers; such branches are picked up, thrown into the fire and burned. If you remain in me and my words remain in you, ask whatever you wish, and it will be done for you. This is to my Father's glory, that you bear much fruit, showing yourselves to be my disciples.

JOHN 15:5–8

WELCOME

Like many large cities in the United States, Philadelphia is home to many wonderful museums. As with most museums, treasured objects and historical artifacts are held behind glass and protected with railings and ropes with posted placards saying, "Do Not Touch."

But one museum is different from the others. The Please Touch Museum is a widely acclaimed children's museum where youngsters learn and explore by utilizing all of their senses. Children are encouraged to take things apart, build new creations, pull things off the shelf, try on costumes and uniforms, and gleefully make a mess. Parents are encouraged to participate as well, learning new things and engaging in new activities right alongside their kids.

While traditional museums have merit, there is a holistic kind of learning that happens in the Please Touch Museum. This study is intended to encourage you to possess the mindset as if you were in the Please Touch Museum. You are invited to participate, engage, be active, use your senses, encounter the passages, take risks, and try new things . . . even if some of the practices feel new and a bit different. In other words, *please touch.*

While most study guides use the phrase "Bible reading" or "Bible study," throughout the Abide Course you will find the phrase that is used is "Scripture engagement." It's one thing to *read* words on a page . . . but quite another to *engage* with the text itself. When you engage with Scripture, you aren't merely reading the words on the page but participating in a relational process where you grasp *these are the words of God from God himself to his people —to you.*

Just as you would get to know someone relationally by listening, interacting, and sharing experiences together, the same is true of Scripture engagement. As Jesus told his disciples, "Abide in me" (John 15:4 ESV). Some scholars translate that word *abide* as meaning *to remain, to dwell,* or *to make your home in.* This is the essence of Scripture engagement.

SHARE

If you or any of your group members are just getting to know one another, take a few minutes to introduce yourselves. Then, to get things started, discuss the following questions:

- What interested you to participate in this study?

- What do you hope to gain from this time during the next several weeks?

WATCH

Watch the video segment for session one. (Play the DVD or see the instructions on the inside front cover on how to access the sessions through streaming). As you watch, use the following outline to record any thoughts or concepts that stand out to you.

Jesus is our source of life and our source of functioning in our Christian lives. As we *abide* in Christ, we are able to bear fruit. We want to be people who are bearing fruit, knowing God, and loving God.

When we come to the Bible, it's a relational process. We come to Scripture to meet and to know God. It keeps us coming back every day because we want to spend time with God.

Scripture engagement and Bible study are two sides of the same coin. We *study* Scripture so that we understand what a passage means—we need to understand what God is saying to us. But then we come back and also *engage* Scripture so that what we read connects to both our hearts and our minds.

The process of engaging Scripture is one we can learn on our own, but the techniques and practices are also powerful to learn from somebody else. We see this taking place in Acts 8, where the Ethiopian eunuch needed the disciple Philip to come alongside of him to help him understand the Scripture.

There are six basic ingredients that go into the process of Scripture engagement:

Ingredient 1: Prepare your heart to be open to the Holy Spirit.

Ingredient 2: Read the Bible.

Ingredient 3: Meditate on the Bible.

Ingredient 4: Talk to God about his Word.

Ingredient 5: Talk about Scriptures with others.

Ingredient 6: Commit to obey what the Word says.

Engaging Scripture is the primary way that we meet Jesus. As he said to the disciples on the road to Emmaus in Luke 24, all the Scriptures point back to him. It's through engaging with the Bible that our eyes will be opened, we will know Jesus, and our hearts will burn for him.

DISCUSS

As you consider what you just watched, use the following questions to discuss these ideas, their basis in Scripture, and their application in your life with your group members.

1. What has your relationship with the Bible been like in the past? Using two or three adjectives, how would you describe that relationship?

2. What would be two or three adjectives that you would *want* to use to describe your relationship with the Bible? Why?

3. Have you ever engaged with Scripture in a way that was deeply transformative and personal as described in this week's teaching? If so, what was it like? What did it feel like? How did it form and shape you?

4. In your own words, how would you articulate the difference between Bible reading, Bible study, and Scripture engagement?

5. Read Psalm 123:1–2. How does this passage describe the way you should approach Scripture? How might that level of focus impact how you engage with the Bible in the weeks ahead? And, in doing so, how might it impact your everyday life?

6. In the teaching, you learned about the six basic "ingredients" for Scripture engagement. Have you engaged in these ingredients before? Are there any elements that have been absent from your approach to Scripture? Explain.

RESPOND

Take a moment to briefly review the notes you took from the teaching. What was one important point that stood out to you?

What is the most important element you learned or thought about for the first time?

What is one thing you can do outside of this group to lean in further with this approach?

PRAY

As you end the session, ask for four people who would be willing to pray briefly and specifically about the following elements:

- *Person 1:* To thank God for bringing together each person in this group and to ask that he would reveal himself to each person.

- *Person 2:* To thank God for the gift of Scripture—and that each member of the group would see it as the precious gift it is.

- *Person 3:* To ask God to surprise you—individually and as a group—during the next several weeks in new, fresh, and exciting ways.

- *Person 4:* To ask God that together you would approach Scripture with expectant hearts, attentive eyes and ears, and a posture of anticipation—and then to have the faith to obey what his Word says.

Personal Practices

Now that you've been introduced to the five Scripture engagement practices that you will be covering during this study, it's time to act on what you've learned. Starting this week, and continuing in the weeks that follow, you will be given five daily exercises to help you participate in the specific Scripture engagement practice that was discussed during your group time. When everyone gathers together again each week, there will be time for you to share briefly what you learned or experienced during this personal time of interaction with God's Word.

In the video teaching for this week, you learned there are six key "ingredients" that go into the process of Scripture engagement. There are different ways to mix and match these ingredients, but the basic core should always be the same:

1. Prepare your heart to be open to the Holy Spirit.
2. Read the Bible and pay attention to what God wants to say to you.
3. Reflect or meditate on what you are reading.

4. Pray—simply talk to God—about the passage.
5. Discuss with others how you are experiencing God in Scripture.
6. Obey what God is instructing you to do through his Word.

To help you get a better understanding of the rhythms of Scripture engagement, the framework of these six ingredients will be used as the structure for this week.

DAY ONE

Prepare your heart to be open to the Holy Spirit.
Take a moment to be still. Open your hands and lay them on your lap in a posture of receiving from God. Close your eyes and take a few slow breaths. After a moment, whisper:

> *Lord, I am here to listen to you today. Speak to me.*

Take a few more slow, full breaths. Then whisper again:

> *Lord, I am here to listen to you today. Speak to me.*

Read John 15:1–8 and pay attention to what God wants to say to you as you read.
Read it slowly and, if your environment is appropriate, consider reading it aloud.

Abide in Christ

Reflect/meditate on what you are reading.

Consider some of these questions as you reflect:

- *What word, thought, or concept sticks out to me?*

- *Is there anything that I need to be reminded of or that I am noticing for the first time in this reading?*

- *What does this passage reveal about the nature or character of Jesus?*

Write down your responses in the space below.

Talk to God about the passage.

Take a few moments to share with God what you are experiencing as you engage with this passage. It may be thanksgiving or praise. It may be a prayer of confession or asking for help. You may want to use these prompts as conversation starters with God:

- *Lord, as I read this, I am feeling . . .*

- *Father, I am being reminded of . . .*

- *Holy Spirit, I sense you want me to step into the truth of this passage by . . .*

- *Jesus, thank you for revealing this to me . . .*

Discuss with others how you are experiencing God in Scripture.
While this is a personal study, is there someone in proximity to you with whom you could share how you experienced this passage—a spouse, child, roommate, friend, or coworker? If so, share one way you experienced this passage in a new or fresh way.

Step out into obedience based on what you've read.
Again, the goal isn't to merely read and learn new information. Instead, the goal is to take what you have gleaned and put it into practice. Answer this question:

> *If I were to lean into the truth of what I received from this passage in one specific and practical way within the next twenty-four hours, what would that look like?*

Write down your response in the space below.

DAY TWO

Prepare your heart to be open to the Holy Spirit.

Open your Bible (or Bible app) to Psalm 86. Place one hand on the place where this passage is found on the page (or on the screen). Put your other hand over your heart. In that posture, take a moment to ask the Lord to move what is on the page to inside of your heart and soul.

Read Psalm 86:11-17 and pay attention to what God wants to say to you as you read.

Read the passage. Then read it a second time, just slightly slower than the first time.

Reflect/meditate on what you are reading.

Consider some of these questions as you reflect:

- *What do I notice?*

- *How does this passage make me feel?*

- *Which verse or line do I believe the Lord wants me to receive today?*

- *Why that particular line or verse?*

Write down your responses in the space below.

Talk to God about the passage.

Share what's on your heart and mind based on what you read. Don't overthink this or "edit" your prayers. God can handle your honesty . . . even if it is raw and messy.

Discuss with others how you are experiencing God in Scripture.

In the space below, record what you have gleaned.

When you gather as a group again later this week, consider sharing what you wrote down.

Step out into obedience based on what you've read.

Answer this question:

> *After engaging with this passage, if I*
> *were to join with Jesus today at home,*
> *at work, or at play, it would be by . . .*

Write down your response in the space below.

DAY THREE

Prepare your heart to be open to the Holy Spirit.
Find a quiet place in your home or office that is free of distraction, noise, and interruption. Close the door. Turn off your screens and put your phone on airplane mode. Then say aloud:

Lord, I am fully yours in this moment.

Read 1 Samuel 3:1-10 and pay attention to what God wants to say to you as you read.
If you are in a quiet, private, and conducive place, read the passage aloud.

Reflect/meditate on what you are reading.
Consider some of these questions as you reflect:

- *What did my ears hear my mouth saying?*

- *Did anything strike me or help me to take notice of a verse or word or phrase?*

- *What must that experience have been like for Samuel to hear God's voice?*

- *Who do I relate to the most in this story?*

Write down your responses in the space below.

Talk to God about the passage.

Just as young Samuel was instructed to say by the priest Eli, say aloud, "*Speak, Lord, for your servant is listening.*" Take a few moments of silence to listen to God. As you hear from him, echo back to him what you sense you received. Consider recording it in the space below.

Discuss with others how you are experiencing God in Scripture.

Consider calling someone in your group and sharing what you gleaned or experienced from your engagement with this passage. Share with them what stuck out to you, or even questions that still remain in your mind. Ask them what they experienced in this passage as well. Write down your responses in the space below.

Step out into obedience based on what you've read.

Answer these questions:

- *What is the invitation from the Lord in this passage in order to join him further this week?*

- *What does that joining together with him look like moving forward today?*

Write down your responses in the space below.

DAY FOUR

Prepare your heart to be open to the Holy Spirit.

Find a place to sit and place your palms on your lap facing up in a posture of openness and receptivity. Say a simple prayer:

*Lord, I am ready to receive what
you have for me today.*

Read Hebrews 4:14–16 and pay attention to what God wants to say to you as you read.

Read the passage in a whisper. Then read it a second time in a low voice. Then read it a third time in your regular volume.

Reflect/meditate on what you are reading.

Consider some of these questions as you reflect:

- *What does this passage say about the character or nature of Jesus?*

- *How does it make you feel that this is who Jesus is?*

Write down your responses in the space below.

Talk to God about the passage.

Take a moment to praise God for who he is and how he has worked through his Son, Jesus.

Discuss with others how you are experiencing God in Scripture.

Who could you share with what you learned during this time? When could you share it with them this week? Write down some thoughts in the space below.

Step out into obedience based on what you've read.

Based on who God is and what you know about his nature, what could it mean for you to approach his throne of grace with confidence (see Hebrews 4:16)? Record your thoughts.

DAY FIVE

Prepare your heart to be open to the Holy Spirit.

Hold your Bible (or Bible app on your phone) in your hands. Breathe slowly and in your spirit ask the Lord to speak to you through his words today.

Read Deuteronomy 6:4-9 and pay attention to what God wants to say to you as you read.

If you are able, read the passage aloud.

Reflect/meditate on what you are reading.

Consider some of these questions as you reflect:

- *Why do you believe God wants his people to be so intentional with his words?*

- *Is there any line or word that you believe is the most important portion to pay attention to in this passage?*

Write down your responses in the space below.

Talk to God about the passage.

Share with God what you are thinking and/or feeling as you read these words. You could also write a brief prayer in the space below.

Discuss with others how you are experiencing God in Scripture.

Who could you share your experience in this passage with today?

Step out into obedience based on what you've read.

What is one way you could join with Jesus today based on what you experienced in this passage? Write your thoughts on this in the space below.

PRAYING SCRIPTURE

Let the message of Christ dwell among you richly as you teach and admonish one another with all wisdom through psalms, hymns, and songs from the Spirit, singing to God with gratitude in your hearts.

COLOSSIANS 3:16

WELCOME

Prayer is great and can feel natural, but it can also be hard and feel dry. Sometimes it may seem that your prayers are passionate and full of life . . . but at other times, they feel distant and limp. Maybe you've felt like you need a boost—or maybe a structure to help assist you.

We have all engaged in the practices of praying and reading Scripture . . . but have you ever engaged in those practices at the same time? Integrating praying and Scripture reading *together* can provide a process and a "skeletal structure" for your connection with God. As we all know, without a healthy skeletal structure present in our physical bodies, we would be nothing more than a blob of skin on the floor, void of shape and unable to move properly. Our skeletal structures give the shape and structure we need to live our lives healthily.

The same is true in our spiritual lives. Praying Scripture can provide shape, and life, and the ability for movement to occur in our relationship with God. We see this demonstrated most clearly in the book of Psalms, which provides a beautiful compilation of prayers right there in the middle of our Bibles. It seems every emotion imaginable is found somewhere in the psalms—joy, anger, loneliness, praise, lament, gratitude, despair, contrition, faithfulness, fear, and more. The psalms give us permission to share our rawest, deepest, and most honest emotions with God, and they can provide a skeletal structure to our engagement with God.

To put it another way, think of praying Scripture like training wheels when you were learning to ride a bike. One training wheel is prayer, and the other is Scripture. When both are installed, they keep you upright and on track to journey in the direction of God's heart.

The beauty of this practice is that it's simple. In short, it's learning to "pray attention" as you read the Bible. You don't need to have a theology degree or be a certified prayer expert to engage with this practice. It just takes a little bit of intentionality and initiative to experience the beauty and power of a deeper connection with God.

SHARE

If you or any of your group members are just getting to know one another, take a few minutes to introduce yourselves. Then, to get things started, discuss the following questions:

- What is one thing you remember from last week's group session—a quote from the teaching, a new idea, an insight, a reminder, a question?

- If you participated in the between-session practices the past week, how did you experience Scripture using all the "ingredients"?

WATCH

Watch the video segment for session two. (Play the DVD or see the instructions on the inside front cover on how to access the sessions through streaming). As you watch, use the following outline to record any thoughts or concepts that stand out to you.

Your sense of being connected with Scripture and with God can deepen as you use the words of the Bible in your prayers. You engage with what you're reading in a personal and immediate way. You then turn that into a conversation with God—with the Holy Spirit guiding the whole process.

If you have followed Christ for any length of time, you've undoubtedly found yourself praying the same prayers over and over again. We all get into ruts at times, and those prayers—if we are honest with ourselves—can start to bore us. But when we use the Bible to guide our prayers, we get out of that rut, start to pray more boldly, and more subjects to pray about enter into our minds.

George Mueller, an evangelist in the 1800s, stumbled on this practice of praying Scripture, and it changed his relationship with God. He would start to pray by praying a simple prayer for God's blessing over his time in the Word. Then he would search the passage for every sort of meaning. He would look at it, ponder the passage, and seek to understand what it was really saying.

We can think of praying Scripture as falling into one of three categories:

Category 1: Praying the prayers of the Bible. There are many prayers in the Bible (such as the Lord's Prayer) and hundreds of others that can become your tutor for how to pray. You can use the words of those specific prayers in the Bible to guide you in your own prayers.

Category 2: Picking a particular topic to pray about. Maybe there is a special need or a specific area in your life that you want to pray over. Different areas or emotions could include being anxious or grumpy or lamenting a loss. There are great prayers and passages in the Bible about a wide variety of topics, and you can use those passages as a guide for your prayers.

Category 3: Paying attention to the Spirit as you read. As you read the stories, history, poems, parables, and everything else in the Bible, you can pay attention to the leading of the Holy Spirit. In doing so, you turn those passages into prayers. This doesn't have to be just about you—you can pray over other people, your church, your community, and even the whole world.

You can pray Scripture with other people. You can do this with just one other person. You can also do it with a small group of people. This can be a great way to help you learn the practice as you hear from other people and the variety of ways they have engaged with the Bible as well.

Praying Scripture is at the heart of Scripture engagement. It's a holistic response to God's Word, rather than just reading words and having them flow in one ear and out the other. When you pray Scripture, it can feel as if you're communicating directly with God as you read and you pray.

DISCUSS

As you consider what you just watched, use the following questions to discuss these ideas, their basis in Scripture, and their application in your life with your group members.

1. In this week's teaching, you learned about three categories of praying Scripture. What were those three categories? Can you give an example of each?

2. Has there been a time when you *prayed the prayers of the Bible*? If so, what was it like? What impact did it have on how you experienced God?

3. When have you *picked a topic to pray about* and then searched the Bible for those prayers? What impact did that have on how you experienced God?

4. Have you ever sought to *pay attention to the Spirit as you read*? What did that look like in your life? What impact did that have on your time with God?

5. Praying Scripture is the essence of Scripture engagement—a holistic response to God's Word rather than just reading the words on the page. How could engaging in praying Scripture help you to abide further with Christ?

6. If prayer is difficult for you, how could this type of engagement with Scripture potentially help you to connect with God in a more relational way?

RESPOND

Take a moment to briefly review the notes you took from the teaching. What do you believe was the most important element for you to take with you in the week ahead?

If you were to try to engage in praying Scripture *on your own* this week, what would your next steps need to be? Be as specific and practical as possible.

If you were to try to engage in praying Scripture *with another person* this week, what would your next steps need to be? Again, be as specific and practical as possible.

Praying Scripture Practice Tips

- Choose a passage that is meaningful to you and speaks truth into your life.
- Take a moment to ask God to bless your time in Scripture, to keep you focused, and to help you pray his Word.
- Start reading through your passage slowly, meditating on each word and verse.
- When you finish reading a verse, stop and turn your thoughts into a prayer.
- Use the words of the Bible to guide your prayers of worship, confession, thanksgiving, and petition for yourself and others.

PRAY

As you close, engage with the Lord's Prayer, found in Matthew 6:9–13, as "training wheels" to help you abide with God together. Ask someone to read the passage aloud while the rest of the group members have their eyes closed. Have the reader pause after each line and encourage each other to vocalize short prayers in the vein of that particular part of the prayer. When this is complete, recite the Lord's Prayer together. Finally, when you get to the line, "*Your kingdom come, your will be done, on earth as it is in heaven,*" have everyone replace the phrase "on earth" with his or her address, neighborhood, city/town, or workplace.

Personal Practices

N ow that you've explored the practice of praying Scripture with your group members, it's time to act on what you've learned. This week, you will be given five daily exercises to help you engage in this Scripture practice and apply what you have learned. When everyone gathers together again next week, there will be time for you to share briefly what you learned or experienced during this personal time of interaction with God's Word.

In the video teaching for this week, you learned there are three primary categories of praying Scripture. These categories are as follows:

- **Category 1: Pray the prayers of the Bible.** There are many prayers throughout the Bible that serve as teaching examples and guides for how to pray.

- **Category 2: Pick a particular topic to pray about.** There are great passages in the Bible on a wide variety of topics that you can turn into your own personalized prayers.

- **Category 3: Pay attention to the Spirit as you read.** As you read a passage—any passage, really—pay attention to the Spirit. In doing so, you can turn those passages into prayers for yourself, for others, or for the world.

This week, you will have the opportunity to engage with each of these three categories by praying Scripture this week.

DAY ONE

Pray the prayers of the Bible (using Psalm 139:1–16).

There are numerous prayers found throughout the Bible, especially in the book of Psalms. For this exercise, you will be reading Psalm 139:1–16. Read the following passage aloud. Read it aloud a second time, but this time, when you get to the pronouns emphasized in bold text, add extra emphasis on the word to make it feel and sound more personal.

> You have searched **me**, LORD,
>   and you know **me**.
> You know when **I** sit and when **I** rise;
>   you perceive **my** thoughts from afar.
> You discern **my** going out and **my** lying down;
>   you are familiar with all **my** ways.
> Before a word is on **my** tongue
>   you, LORD, know it completely.
> You hem **me** in behind and before,

Praying Scripture

*and you lay your hand upon **me**.*
*Such knowledge is too wonderful for **me**,*
> *too lofty for **me** to attain.*

*Where can **I** go from your Spirit?*
> *Where can **I** flee from your presence?*
*If **I** go up to the heavens, you are there;*
> *if **I** make my bed in the depths, you are there.*
*If **I** rise on the wings of the dawn,*
> *if **I** settle on the far side of the sea,*
*even there your hand will guide **me**,*
> *your right hand will hold **me** fast.*
*If I say, "Surely the darkness will hide **me***
> *and the light become night around **me**,"*
even the darkness will not be dark to you;
> *the night will shine like the day,*
> *for darkness is as light to you.*

*For you created **my** inmost being;*
> *you knit **me** together in **my** mother's womb.*
I praise you because I am fearfully and wonderfully made;
> *your works are wonderful,*
> *I know that full well.*
***My** frame was not hidden from you*
> *when I was made in the secret place,*
> *when I was woven together in the depths of the earth.*
*Your eyes saw **my** unformed body;*
> *all the days ordained for **me** were written in your book*
> *before one of them came to be.*

When you are finished, simply say aloud:

Lord, hear my prayer. Amen.

DAY TWO

Pray the prayers of the Bible (using Psalm 51:1-19).

For this exercise, you will be reading Psalm 51:1-19, which scholars believe King David wrote when the prophet Nathan confronted him about his adultery with Bathsheba. Read the following passage aloud slowly, carefully, and prayerfully. Read it again, but this time when you sense a verse or phrase is speaking directly to you, pause for a moment before you continue reading. If there is something that comes to mind as you read—a specific sin or a shortcoming in your life—confess it to God. Ask for his forgiveness and grace in that area of your life.

> *Have mercy on me, O God,*
> *   according to your unfailing love;*
> *according to your great compassion*
> *   blot out my transgressions.*
> *Wash away all my iniquity*
> *   and cleanse me from my sin.*
> *For I know my transgressions,*
> *   and my sin is always before me.*
> *Against you, you only, have I sinned*
> *   and done what is evil in your sight;*
> *so you are right in your verdict*
> *   and justified when you judge.*

Praying Scripture

surely I was sinful at birth,
*   sinful from the time my mother conceived me.*
Yet you desired faithfulness even in the womb;
*   you taught me wisdom in that secret place.*
Cleanse me with hyssop, and I will be clean;
*   wash me, and I will be whiter than snow.*
Let me hear joy and gladness;
*   let the bones you have crushed rejoice.*
Hide your face from my sins
*   and blot out all my iniquity.*
Create in me a pure heart, O God,
*   and renew a steadfast spirit within me.*
Do not cast me from your presence
*   or take your Holy Spirit from me.*
Restore to me the joy of your salvation
*   and grant me a willing spirit, to sustain me.*
Then I will teach transgressors your ways,
*   so that sinners will turn back to you.*
Deliver me from the guilt of bloodshed, O God,
*   you who are God my Savior,*
*   and my tongue will sing of your righteousness.*
Open my lips, Lord,
*   and my mouth will declare your praise.*
You do not delight in sacrifice, or I would bring it;
*   you do not take pleasure in burnt offerings.*
My sacrifice, O God, is a broken spirit;
*   a broken and contrite heart*
*   you, God, will not despise.*
May it please you to prosper Zion,
*   to build up the walls of Jerusalem.*

Then you will delight in the sacrifices of the righteous,
in burnt offerings offered whole;
then bulls will be offered on your altar.

After reading this psalm, pause, be still, and listen for anything you sense the Lord is saying to you. Before concluding, whisper a simple prayer:

God, thank you for forgiving me. Amen.

DAY THREE

Pick a particular topic to pray about (using various passages).
There are great passages in the Bible on a wide variety of topics that you can turn into your own personalized prayers. Consider where you are emotionally or what you might be feeling in your current state. Maybe you feel one of the following emotions:

- Grateful

- Fearful or anxious

- Discouraged

- Guilty or feeling the need to confess sin

- In need of help

Praying Scripture

- Angry

- Lonely

If one of these emotions describes what you are currently feeling, pick one or two of the corresponding passages listed below to read slowly, carefully, and prayerfully. Personalize them. Digest them into your soul. Maybe you want to write out these verses on a piece of paper where you can see them at the start of each day or in a journal. As you write them, use that time of slowing down to reflect and engage with God in the process.

- Grateful: Psalm 116:17–19; Ephesians 5:18–20; 1 Thessalonians 5:18

- Fearful or anxious: Psalm 27:1–6; Isaiah 41:10; Philippians 4:6–7

- Discouraged: Deuteronomy 31:1–6; John 16:33; Galatians 6:9

- Guilty or feeling the need to confess sin: Psalm 32:5; Romans 5:1; 1 John 1:9

- In need of help: Psalm 46:1–3; Hebrews 4:15–16; James 1:5

- Angry: Proverbs 14:29; Ephesians 4:26; James 1:19

- Lonely: Psalm 27:10; John 14:17; 1 Peter 5:7

After you have prayed these passages, write in the space below what you sense you experienced with God during this time.

DAY FOUR

Pay attention to the Spirit as you read (using Luke 9:23-27). Praying Scripture allows you to take any passage and simply read it while paying attention to what the Holy Spirit is impressing on your heart. So today, take a moment to pause and just be still. Ask the Lord to guide your time in Scripture. Simply say:

Lord, surprise me with what you want to show me today.

Now read Luke 9:23-27 slowly. As you read, think about what the Lord would want you to personally receive in this passage. Record it below.

Praying Scripture

Now re-read the passage and think about what the Holy Spirit may want to impress on you as it relates to the people you know (your family, friends, colleagues, coworkers, neighbors, fellow students, and the like). Who comes to your mind as you read this passage? Write their names down and pray specifically for them.

Finally, read the passage a third time. This time, consider what implications the words you are reading might have for the entire world. Think about different continents, countries, and cultures. Does a particular country or people group come to mind as you read? Intercede for them. Pray that God would reveal himself more fully to people in that country or region of the world. Record your thoughts on this experience below.

DAY FIVE

Pay attention to the Spirit as you read (using James 3:1–12).
Once again, take a moment to pause and just be still. Ask the
Lord to guide your time in Scripture. Simply say:

> *Lord, open my heart to receive what*
> *you want to show me today.*

Read James 3:1–12 aloud. Pay attention to what stands out to
you from the passage: a challenge, a reminder, an encouragement, a conviction about something. Write it below.

What metaphor helps you understand what James is saying
about the power of the tongue?

Praying Scripture

Re-read the passage. Ask the Holy Spirit to speak to you based on what you're reading. Now finish this sentence: *After I read this passage, I sense the Lord wants me to live faithfully today by* . . . Record your thoughts in the space below.

End by asking God to grant you the faith needed to honor him and others with your words.

ENGAGE THROUGH ART

When I consider your heavens, the work of your fingers, the moon and the stars, which you have set in place, what is mankind that you are mindful of them, human beings that you care for them?

PSALM 8:3–4

WELCOME

You're probably familiar with the three learning styles—*visual*, *auditory*, and *kinesthetic*. Visual learners "see" abstract concepts in their head through diagrams or word pictures. They may draw diagrams on a whiteboard to understand a truth or scribble on a napkin to explain something to others in a way that they can understand.

Auditory learners are those who hear a song once and then can sit down at a piano and pound out the tune. They prefer audio books to traditional ones. Kinesthetic learners are at their best when they can use materials to build a tangible model. They learn more on "field trips" experiencing the world than they do in a classroom or company boardroom.

Regardless of your particular learning style—or what you believe about your own creative abilities—God has purposefully created you in his image and has called you to be a co-creator with him. Maybe you are one of those rare individuals who considers himself or herself to be an artist or poet or musician or sculptor—at least in the traditional sense of the word. But the truth is that we *all* have a creative spark in us. It may take the form of brainstorming creative solutions to problems, teaching others how to solve equations, or organizing important data in a new way to present it clearly to our team at work. This is all creative work!

So don't let the title of this session put you off. You don't have to be an artist in the traditional sense of the word to engage in this next Scripture engagement practice. Rather, you can engage with Scripture more deeply by simply reflecting on the works of art that Christians have expressed over the ages to relate the stories and concepts of Scripture in a beautiful way. So, open up your mind . . . and get ready to embrace your more "artistic" side!

SHARE

To get things started for this week, discuss the following questions:

- If you participated in the between-session practices the past week, which "category" of praying Scripture resonated with you the most? Why?

- Is there an art piece that has changed the way you viewed or understood Scripture? If so, which one? How has it changed your understanding?

WATCH

Watch the video segment for session three. (Play the DVD or see the instructions on the inside front cover on how to access the sessions through streaming). As you watch, use the following outline to record any thoughts or concepts that stand out to you.

Sometimes, people in the church are a little hesitant to connect with artists and their artwork. Yet in the very first verse in the

Bible, we read, "In the beginning God created the heavens and the earth" (Genesis 1:1). We see that God himself is a *creator* and that he is an *artist*.

In the book of Exodus, we read how God called Bezalel and filled him "with the Spirit of God, with wisdom, with understanding" to make the tabernacle beautiful (31:3). The tabernacle, and the artwork in the tabernacle, helped people meet and to know God. It became the center of Israel's worship.

Emotionally, our faith is both about our thinking and our feeling, and art can help us to bring those two together. Images can be powerful triggers to help us both remember the stories and the truths of the Bible and to be motivated toward obedience. Art can be used as a tool for spiritual growth for everyone.

Typical Bible commentators read a passage to understand its language, context, history, and theology, and then help us understand the message of the passage and what it is saying. But artists help us to not only understand what a passage *means* but also how it should impact our lives *emotionally*.

The goal of Scripture engagement is not to just gather information about the Bible but to slow down and realize that God wants us to use the Scriptures to meet him. We let the Holy Spirit question our lives through the words he inspired so that we can yield to God and be transformed into his image.

You don't have to do this practice just by yourself. You can gather other people around you—and they will see things in a painting or other work of art that you don't see and make connections to a passage.

DISCUSS

As you consider what you just watched, use the following questions to discuss these ideas, their basis in Scripture, and their application in your life with your group members.

1. Read aloud Genesis 1:1; Exodus 35:35; and Ecclesiastes 3:11. Many people in the church today are often hesitant to connect with artists and their works connected to the Bible. But what do these passages say about God as a creator and artist?

2. Look at *The Calling of Matthew* painting by Caravaggio reprinted on the next page in this guide. As you reflect on the painting, is there anything else that stands out to you that was not covered in this week's teaching? If so, what stands out?

3. What are your initial reactions to this practice? What are some of the creative gifts that you believe God has provided to you? How are you using those gifts?

4. The goal of Scripture engagement is not just to gather more information but to slow down and see that God wants to meet you in the Scriptures—and in your own life. How might this particular practice help you to slow down and "see" God?

5. Emotionally, our faith is both about thinking *and* feeling. Why is it important to engage with Scripture using not only your head (knowledge) but also your heart (emotions)?

6. If you are an artist, what Scripture passage or biblical story might you choose to create something yourself in the near future? (If you engage in this, would you consider bringing it in the next week or two to allow the group to see what you created?)

RESPOND

Take a moment to briefly review the notes you took from the teaching. What do you believe was the most important element for you to take with you in the week ahead?

If you were to engage Scripture through art on *your own* this week, what would your next steps need to be? Be as specific and practical as possible.

If you were to engage Scripture through art *with another person* this week, what would your next steps need to be? Again, be as specific and practical as possible.

Engage Through Art Practice Tips

- Find a good source of quality biblical artwork. This might be a book, a website, or even a museum. Look for art that intrigues you personally and helps you gain a deeper understanding of the Scripture passage you are interested in exploring.
- Take time to reflect on the piece of art. Ask yourself these questions:
  - What is the artist portraying?
  - How are light, color, and lines used?
  - What figures from the biblical account are portrayed?
  - How do they react to what is going on?
  - How do they appear to relate to each other?
  - What figures do I most connect with?
  - Why do I connect with a particular figure?
  - How does this piece help me connect with the Bible story on a deeper level?
  - How is God at work in this event?
- Familiarize yourself with the passage that corresponds with the artwork. Let the work of the artist drive you deeper into your reflection of God's Word.
- Ask God to direct your experience. Pray that the Holy Spirit will give you wisdom and discernment as you seek to discover new truths about him and how he works in the lives of his people. Consider journaling about your experience.

- Finally, consider making your own piece of biblical art! You will engage with a passage at a deeper level as you strive to visually represent a Bible passage.

PRAY

Close by taking a moment to thank God for the sense of sight. Briefly express your gratitude aloud for the artists throughout the centuries (including Caravaggio) who brought biblical stories to life through art, and those who continue to do so today. Finally, ask God to provide fresh insight and new vision to help you see art and connect it to Scripture for deeper understanding and encounters with God in the coming week.

SESSION THREE

Personal Practices

N ow that you've explored the practice of engaging Scripture through art with your group members, it's time to act on what you've learned. This week, you will be given five daily exercises to help you engage in this Scripture practice and apply what you have learned. When everyone gathers together again next week, there will be time for you to share briefly what you learned or experienced during this personal time of interaction with God's Word.

This week, you will need to have access to the internet so that you can search for the different art pieces that are mentioned. While it's normally best to put screens away so you can be fully attentive, focused, and present . . . you will need to use those screens for these exercises!

DAY ONE

Daniel in the Lion's Den *and* Daniel's Answer to the King *by Briton Riviere*

Read Daniel 6:10-23, and then search online for *Daniel in the Lion's Den* by Briton Riviere (1872). As you look at this work of art, slowly take in each detail, making sure that your eyes move over every part of the piece. What connection do you see between the painting and what you read in the passage?

What detail or details stick out to you the most (the eyes of the lion, the bones on the floor, the relaxed shoulders of Daniel)? Write those below.

Now re-read verses 18-22 of the passage, and then do another online search for a second painting by Riviere called *Daniel's Answer to the King* (1890). What do you notice in this second piece? Does anything surprise you?

Engage Through Art

How do Riviere's two pieces help you see the passage with greater perception, depth, thought, and emotion?

Do these have any implications on how you respond to this story in your own life? Explain.

End in prayer, thanking God for Daniel's determined faith in spite of the circumstances. Ask God to grant you the same kind of determined faith and trust in him.

DAY TWO

The Annunciation *by Henry Ossawa*

Read Luke 2:26–38, and then search online for *The Annunciation* by Henry Ossawa Tanner (1898). As you look at this work of art, slowly take in each detail, making sure that your eyes move over every part of the piece. Again, take in each detail and explore every part of the piece. What do you notice about the look on Mary's face? What do you think she is feeling?

What do you notice about the depiction of the angel bringing Mary the news?

What thoughts or emotions do you have as you look at this piece?

Does this piece help you understand the passage with greater thought or perspective? If so, how? Record it in the space below.

Now, with this piece in your mind, slowly and prayerfully read Luke 2:26-38 again. Thank God for the faithful and joyful response of Mary to the news that the Savior would be born—and pray that you would also respond in obedience as the Lord speaks to you.

Finally, consider sharing a work of art with one or two other people today. Discuss with them what you experienced in this practice. Ask for their responses to the painting as well.

DAY THREE

Massacre of the Innocents *by Léon Cogniet*

Yesterday, you looked at Henry Ossawa Tanner's painting *The Annunciation*. After the announcement of Mary's pregnancy and the hope-filled arrival of Christ, chaos and violence ensued due to the evil and violent edict of King Herod to murder the baby boys in Bethlehem. Read Matthew 2:16–18, and then search online for "Scene du Massacre des Innocents" by Léon Cogniet (1824). Take in each detail and explore every part of the piece. Notice the piercing eyes of the mother. What might she be feeling in that moment? (Notice, too, her hands over the mouth of her son.) What does her look make you feel as she stares directly at you?

Notice the chaos ensuing in the background. What might this scene have sounded like?

If you could ask the artist one or two questions about the painting, what would you ask?

Read Matthew 2:16–18 again, and then respond to God with whatever is in your heart.

DAY FOUR

Christ of Saint John of the Cross *by Salvador Dalí*

Read Matthew 27:45-50, and then search online for *Christ of Saint John of the Cross* by Salvador Dalí (1951). Take in each detail and explore every part of the piece. What do you notice about this painting of Jesus' crucifixion? How is this angle and line of vision different than most other paintings of Jesus on the cross?

Dalí wants the viewer to see the crucifixion from God's perspective up above the earth. What might God have been feeling as he watched his beloved Son's death on the cross?

What might that tell you about the heart and character of God?

Read Matthew 27:45-50 again (aloud if you can). Pause for a moment and consider God's view of the greatest moment of redemption the world has ever experienced. Share with him whatever thoughts that come to mind. It may be confession, praise, or gratitude.

DAY FIVE

The Incredulity of Saint Thomas *by Caravaggio*

During the teaching this week, you examined a painting by the Italian baroque painter Caravaggio titled *The Calling of Saint Matthew*. Now read John 20:24-34 and search online for another Caravaggio painting titled "The Incredulity of Saint Thomas" (1601-1602). Take in each detail and explore every part of the piece. What is your initial reaction to the painting? Awe? Disgust? Joy? Serenity? Are you moved in any way by what you see?

Baroque painters like Caravaggio skillfully used light to draw viewers' eyes toward certain details in their pieces. Where is the light focused in this painting? On what—or who—are your eyes drawn?

Notice the faces in the painting—the eyes, the furrowed brows, the expressions. How would you describe each one of them?

Now notice each of the hands. Could they tell you anything about what each person might be feeling in that moment?

Think about the times—in the past or maybe even the present— where you have experienced doubt. Put yourself in the position of Thomas in the painting. What would you feel as Jesus was focusing his attention on you and pursuing you? How might Jesus speak to your doubts?

With this message fresh in your mind, re-read the passage. Now, with your eyes open and looking intently at the painting, pray aloud whatever is on your heart—whether confession, praise, thanksgiving, or a petition to God.

These commandments that I give you today are to be on your hearts. Impress them on your children. Talk about them when you sit at home and when you walk along the road, when you lie down and when you get up. Tie them as symbols on your hands and bind them on your foreheads. Write them on the doorframes of your houses and on your gates.

DEUTERONOMY 6:6-9

WELCOME

"Do you have a pen I can borrow?" Maybe you've asked this of a friend or coworker or had someone ask this of you. There are moments in the week where you just need to jot down something important so you don't forget. Or write down something to make sure you get your thoughts out so you can more clearly understand what you are thinking or feeling.

Some people are natural notetakers. They have a pen with them at all times and a journal in which they write each morning. Others of us . . . not so much. Fortunately, there is no command in Scripture that states, "Thou shalt journal every day." And other than one instance of Jesus stooping down and writing in the sand, he wasn't much of a journaller himself.

In our current digital age, sitting down to write with pen and paper is less common (and more time consuming), but there's something valuable about the process that can help you tap into something important. You experience things differently when writing it out by hand than when you tap it out on your phone or laptop. In fact, one of the benefits of the pen-to-paper handwriting process is that it will intentionally slow you down. In a world that prioritizes speed and efficiency, sometimes being forced to slow down—even if only for a few brief moments—can provide you with clearer focus on what you're thinking and feeling. It can help you be more fully present in the moment rather than rushing off to do the next thing.

Even if you don't find that journaling comes naturally to you, be open to engaging with this practice this week. Don't worry about the quality of your penmanship, the accuracy of your spelling and grammar, the pace at which you write, or how articulate you think you should be. (In this exercise, nobody will force you to share what you write.) Just focus on taking what is on your mind and heart and moving it onto the page. Sure, your hand might become tired and you may find yourself growing impatient by how slow the process might be. But you may be surprised by what you learn and how you experience God in new ways because of it.

SHARE

To get things started for this week, discuss the following questions:

- If you participated in the between-session practices the past week, which work of art stood out to you the most? How did it help you to engage further and deeper with the accompanying Scripture passage you read?

- How often do you engage in a regular practice of journaling? If you frequently journal, how has it benefited your spiritual life? If you don't frequently journal, why do you think the practice is difficult or unhelpful to you?

WATCH

Watch the video segment for session four. (Play the DVD or see the instructions on the inside front cover on how to access the sessions through streaming). As you watch, use the following outline to record any thoughts or concepts that stand out to you.

Scripture journaling is the practice of reading the Bible and then prayerfully writing out your thoughts, feelings, prayers, and other reactions you have to the passage. As you put your thoughts on paper, it helps you to think more deeply about the passage and about your life.

Writing things down just makes you think them through at a deeper level. All writing helps you clarify what you are thinking, what you are feeling, and what you do and do not understand.

You don't have to be a writer to use this Scripture engagement practice. It's just a conversation that you are having with God. A Scripture journal is a place where you can safely record and reflect on your raw thoughts and feelings that come up as you read the Bible.

As with all Scripture engagement practices, but especially with journaling, there is more than one way to do this. But here is a basic outline that may be helpful for how to begin your approach.

Prepare your heart to be with God. You could sing a song or say a prayer—even something as simple as, "Okay, I'm going to focus in on you, God."

Write a bit about your day or what you're feeling. This will expose your mind and heart to God and is an effective way to corral your thinking.

Pray about what you wrote. Just tell God, "Lord, this is how I feel. But in the end, I want to end up thinking your thoughts about everything that I'm thinking and feeling."

Read a passage from the Bible. You could use a Bible reading plan (many are found on the internet) or follow along with what your church is currently studying (or studied in the past).

Write down anything that stands out to you after reading the passage. Ask yourself, "What would my life look like if I responded to the truth I just read? What changes could that make in my life?" Write down any prayers—confession, gratitude, praise—or record a potential action step or next step of obedience to take based on the passage you read.

Journaling is primarily private—you're writing for yourself and talking to God. But it can also be done with a small group perhaps. Read a passage, journal about it, and then share afterward.

Scripture journaling is a powerful process. There are many resources out there that can help you journal Scripture. Some of them are online and some are in print. Give this powerful practice a try!

DISCUSS

As you consider what you just watched, use the following questions to discuss these ideas, their basis in Scripture, and their application in your life with your group members.

1. Do you agree with the statement made in this week's teaching that writing things down helps you to clarify what you are really thinking or feeling? Why or why not?

2. Do you have any fears that you are "not a good enough writer" to engage in this practice? How did this week's teaching help to diminish those concerns?

3. What might be the potential benefits of engaging with Scripture by journaling? How could that enhance and deepen the way you connect with God each day?

4. If you have found journaling to be beneficial, what process do you follow in terms of the length of time you write, the frequency of when you write, where you write, and the time of day you journal? How did you arrive at what worked best for you?

5. Read aloud Psalm 88:1-5. What are some of the emotions the psalmist is "journaling" about in these verses? What does he nevertheless acknowledge about God?

6. Read aloud 2 Timothy 3:16-17. The Bible is "God's Word"—a message to those who desire to serve him—as recorded by his faithful followers across many centuries. What does this passage say about the power of that written Word?

RESPOND

Take a moment to briefly review the notes you took from the teaching. What do you believe was the most important element for you to take with you in the week ahead?

If you were to try to engage in journaling *on your own* this week, what would your next steps need to be? Be as specific and practical as possible.

If you were to try to engage in journaling *with another person* this week, what would your next steps need to be? Again, be as specific and practical as possible.

Journaling Scripture Practice Tips:
- Choose a time and place for journaling that is comfortable and free of distractions. Simple things like a comfortable chair, sitting up straight, and good lighting can all make a difference.
- Use your journal to clear your mind of distracting thoughts before diving into Scripture. Write down any worries or distractions, perhaps as a prayer, as a way of giving them over to God before you begin reading.
- Express your heart to God in whatever way best suits you. If you are a visual learner, try writing with different colored pens and markers, doodling, or creating your own drawings to depict a Scripture passage or story.

- Be honest with yourself and God in your writing and make sure that others respect the privacy of your journal. It is important that you are able to write without worrying about who else might read it.
- Don't become overly dependent on your journal. If you are prone to over-journaling, set a time limit for yourself before you begin.

PRAY

As you conclude, allow time and space for everyone in the group to journal a two- to four-sentence prayer. The prayer could be one of gratitude, or asking God for his help with a problem that you are currently facing, or a request for God to intercede in the life of someone you know. Ask those who are willing to share what they wrote to close out your time together.

Personal Practices

Now that you've explored the practice of journaling with your group members, it's time to act on what you've learned. This week, you will be given five daily exercises to help you engage in this Scripture practice and apply what you have learned. When everyone gathers together again next week, there will be time for you to share briefly what you learned or experienced during this personal time of interaction with God's Word.

If you already write regularly in a journal or diary . . . that is great. Feel free to continue that practice in place of these exercises or just incorporate these exercises into your typical journaling time. If you don't regularly write in a journal . . . you may want to consider securing one. It doesn't need to be expensive or fancy—it can be as simple as a spiral notebook or even a few pages of lined notebook paper. (Note that for this week's personal practices, ample space has been included in this study guide for you to journal.)

DAY ONE

Journal using John 10:1–18.

Remember the format shared during this week's teaching. First, *prepare your heart to be with God.* You could sing a song, say a prayer—even just something like, "Okay, I'm going to focus in on you, God." Next, *write a bit about your day—about what you're thinking or feeling.* This is an effective way to focus your heart and mind during this time. Use the space below to do this.

Finally, pray a brief prayer. Keep this simple: "Lord, this is how I feel. But in the end, I want to end up thinking your thoughts about everything that I'm thinking and feeling." Now that your heart and mind are primed to listen and engage, read these words from John 10:1–18:

> *"Very truly I tell you Pharisees, anyone who does not enter the sheep pen by the gate, but climbs in by some other way, is a thief and a robber. The one who enters by the gate is the shepherd of the sheep. The gatekeeper opens the gate for him, and the sheep listen to his voice. He calls his own sheep*

by name and leads them out. When he has brought out all his own, he goes on ahead of them, and his sheep follow him because they know his voice. But they will never follow a stranger; in fact, they will run away from him because they do not recognize a stranger's voice." Jesus used this figure of speech, but the Pharisees did not understand what he was telling them.

Therefore Jesus said again, "Very truly I tell you, I am the gate for the sheep. All who have come before me are thieves and robbers, but the sheep have not listened to them. I am the gate; whoever enters through me will be saved. They will come in and go out, and find pasture. The thief comes only to steal and kill and destroy; I have come that they may have life, and have it to the full.

"I am the good shepherd. The good shepherd lays down his life for the sheep. The hired hand is not the shepherd and does not own the sheep. So when he sees the wolf coming, he abandons the sheep and runs away. Then the wolf attacks the flock and scatters it. The man runs away because he is a hired hand and cares nothing for the sheep.

"I am the good shepherd; I know my sheep and my sheep know me—just as the Father knows me and I know the Father— and I lay down my life for the sheep. I have other sheep that are not of this sheep pen. I must bring them also. They too will listen to my voice, and there shall be one flock and one shepherd. The reason my Father loves me is that I lay down my life—only to take it up again. No one takes it from me, but I lay it down of my own accord. I have authority to lay it down and authority to take it up again. This command I received from my Father."

What truth in this passage—a verse, a phrase, a sentence, a word—stands out to you? Take your pen and circle or underline that truth and put a date next to it in the margin. Next, in the space below, write out two or three questions that you have about the passage.

If you were there with Jesus listening to what he was saying, what would you be feeling as you heard his words?

If you heard Jesus finish this teaching, what do you think your response might have been? What do you think your response should be right now?

Journal

Finish the prompts:

Lord, I sense you want me to know that you are . . .

Jesus, after reading this, I sense you are inviting me to . . .

Look back over what you have written. Underline or put a star by what you believe to be the most important points from your journaling.

DAY TWO

Journal using Psalm 121:1-8.

At the top of your journal, or in the space provided below, write out a one-sentence prayer of your desire for God to reveal himself to you during this time. Once again, it could be something simple like: "Lord, in this time, show me something new about who you are."

Now read Psalm 121 slowly. When you are finished, read it a second time, pausing between each verse for a moment before beginning again.

I lift up my eyes to the mountains—
*   where does my help come from?*
My help comes from the LORD,
*   the Maker of heaven and earth.*

He will not let your foot slip—
*   he who watches over you will not slumber;*
indeed, he who watches over Israel
*   will neither slumber nor sleep.*

The LORD watches over you—
*   the LORD is your shade at your right hand;*
the sun will not harm you by day,
*   nor the moon by night.*

Journal

The LORD will keep you from all harm—
  he will watch over your life;
the LORD will watch over your coming and going
  both now and forevermore.

Notice the words in this psalm about *vision* (seeing, looking, watching) and about *harm, safety,* and *protection.* Circle all these words. What might the psalmist have been feeling as he recorded this song? What might have been his primary emotions, concerns, or fears?

What would your life look like if you responded to the truth of what you just read? What changes could that make in your life?

What questions do you have about the passage? Where does your curiosity rise?

What do you need to be reminded of from this passage regarding God's character?

Finish by writing out a prayer based on what you read. It could be a prayer of praise (for God being your protector), for provision (that God would protect you in a specific situation), or of confession (telling God about your fear or lack of trust in his goodness).

DAY THREE

Journal using Matthew 6:25–34.

Take a moment to ask God to move in your head, heart, soul—and even your hand and fingers—during this time. Leave a moment or two of silence. Then simply say, "Amen." Now read the following words from Jesus found in Matthew 6:25–34:

> "Therefore I tell you, do not worry about your life, what you will eat or drink; or about your body, what you will wear. Is not life more than food, and the body more than clothes? Look at the birds of the air; they do not sow or reap or store away in barns, and yet your heavenly Father feeds them. Are you not much more valuable than they? Can any one of you by worrying add a single hour to your life?
>
> "And why do you worry about clothes? See how the flowers of the field grow. They do not labor or spin. Yet I tell you that not even Solomon in all his splendor was dressed like one of these. If that is how God clothes the grass of the field, which is here today and tomorrow is thrown into the fire, will he not much more clothe you—you of little faith? So do not worry, saying, 'What shall we eat?' or 'What shall we drink?' or 'What shall we wear?' For the pagans run after all these things, and your heavenly Father knows that you need them. But seek first his kingdom and his righteousness, and all these things will be given to you as well. Therefore do not worry about tomorrow, for tomorrow will worry about itself. Each day has enough trouble of its own."

The Abide Bible Course

In this portion of the Sermon on the Mount, Jesus asked several questions of his listeners—many of them rhetorical in nature. Which question sticks out to you the most (out of encouragement, challenge, or intrigue)? Write it below.

Jesus uses a number of images, visuals, and objects to drive home his point to not worry (food, clothing, birds, barns, flowers, grass, fire). Which image rises to the surface of your mind? Why that image in particular?

Which verse do you believe you most need to receive at this time? In the space below, write out that verse. As you write it slowly, hold a prayerful posture with each letter of each word.

Journal

Imagine Jesus speaking these words directly to you in a one-on-one conversation. What would you be feeling or experiencing? What questions would you have for him? What do you believe you should do after that conversation was over? Write your thoughts and reflections below.

Read the passage again. Then finish this prompt. *Jesus, I thank you for . . .*

DAY FOUR

Journal using Numbers 21:4–9 and John 3:1–16.

Start by simply stating, "Lord, speak to me today. I am listening." Now read the following story found in Numbers 21:4–9:

> They traveled from Mount Hor along the route to the Red Sea, to go around Edom. But the people grew impatient on the way; they spoke against God and against Moses, and said, "Why have you brought us up out of Egypt to die in the wilderness? There is no bread! There is no water! And we detest this miserable food!"
>
> Then the LORD sent venomous snakes among them; they bit the people and many Israelites died. The people came

*to Moses and said, "We sinned when we spoke against the
LORD and against you. Pray that the LORD will take the snakes
away from us." So Moses prayed for the people.*

*The LORD said to Moses, "Make a snake and put it up
on a pole; anyone who is bitten can look at it and live." So
Moses made a bronze snake and put it up on a pole. Then
when anyone was bitten by a snake and looked at the bronze
snake, they lived.*

List three to five questions below that you have about the passage. These may be questions such as, What did the bronze snake look like? Or, Why did God provide the people with an opportunity to look at the snake in order to receive healing?

If you were the Israelites, what would you be thinking or feeling in this story?

Journal

Now read Jesus' interaction with Nicodemus in John 3:1–16:

Now there was a Pharisee, a man named Nicodemus who was a member of the Jewish ruling council. He came to Jesus at night and said, "Rabbi, we know that you are a teacher who has come from God. For no one could perform the signs you are doing if God were not with him."

Jesus replied, "Very truly I tell you, no one can see the kingdom of God unless they are born again."

"How can someone be born when they are old?" Nicodemus asked. "Surely they cannot enter a second time into their mother's womb to be born!"

Jesus answered, "Very truly I tell you, no one can enter the kingdom of God unless they are born of water and the Spirit. Flesh gives birth to flesh, but the Spirit gives birth to spirit. You should not be surprised at my saying, 'You must be born again.' The wind blows wherever it pleases. You hear its sound, but you cannot tell where it comes from or where it is going. So it is with everyone born of the Spirit."

"How can this be?" Nicodemus asked.

"You are Israel's teacher," said Jesus, "and do you not understand these things? Very truly I tell you, we speak of what we know, and we testify to what we have seen, but still you people do not accept our testimony. I have spoken to you of earthly things and you do not believe; how then will you believe if I speak of heavenly things? No one has ever gone into heaven except the one who came from heaven—the Son of Man. Just as Moses lifted up the snake in the wilderness, so the Son of Man must be lifted up, that everyone who believes may have eternal life in him."

For God so loved the world that he gave his one and only Son, that whoever believes in him shall not perish but have eternal life.

Why do you think Jesus mentioned the incident with the snakes in verses 14 and 15?

What does that tell you about who Jesus is and why he came to earth?

Write a few final thoughts, questions, or reflections you may have about the connection between these two stories.

Now write any implications these stories have for you and how you see Jesus.

DAY FIVE

Journal using Proverbs 8:1-11

Once again, take a moment to ask God to move in your head, heart, soul, hand, and fingers during this time. Leave a moment or two of silence. Now read Proverbs 8:1-11:

Does not wisdom call out?
Does not understanding raise her voice?
At the highest point along the way,
where the paths meet, she takes her stand;
beside the gate leading into the city,
at the entrance, she cries aloud:
"To you, O people, I call out;
I raise my voice to all mankind.
You who are simple, gain prudence;
you who are foolish, set your hearts on it.
Listen, for I have trustworthy things to say;
I open my lips to speak what is right.
My mouth speaks what is true,

> *for my lips detest wickedness.*
> *All the words of my mouth are just;*
>> *none of them is crooked or perverse.*
> *To the discerning all of them are right;*
>> *they are upright to those who have found knowledge.*
> *Choose my instruction instead of silver,*
>> *knowledge rather than choice gold,*
> *for wisdom is more precious than rubies,*
>> *and nothing you desire can compare with her.*

This passage is the personification of wisdom. What do you notice about Lady Wisdom? What is she doing? List these actions below.

What does Lady Wisdom want listeners to do? How does she want them to respond?

Journal

Read verses 10 and 11 again. In the space below, write out these verses by hand. And as you do, pray as you write each word.

As you wrote, how were your prayers directed? Toward yourself? For a family member or friend? For those in your church? Record a thought or two from your prayer.

Finally, finish this sentence: *Lord, today I want to respond to wisdom's call by* . . .

PICTURE IT

*Taste and see that the L*ORD *is good;*
blessed is the one who takes refuge in him.

PSALM 34:8

WELCOME

Many high performing athletes rely on sports psychologists in their training regimen to maximize their performance. These trained specialists help athletes visualize their moves long before they take the field or step onto the court. They encourage athletes to slow down, close their eyes, "see" the field or court, hear the crowd, envision their competition, and observe and decide how they will move and react in various situations.

The purpose of this process is to have the athletes envision the plays and make decisions *before* they happen. In this way, when they are actually in the moment, they will be able to perform in what is called a state of "flow." Many athletes who participate in these exercises describe that they experience the actual game in "slow motion"—and are thus able to perform and react much more effectively because of the preliminary work they have done.

Maybe you've prepared to give a speech or presentation by visualizing the audience listening to your talk. You imagined the facial expressions of the group or anticipated the questions you might receive. Or maybe you've pictured yourself performing in a sold-out concert hall or music venue. You've envisioned what you will be wearing, how your fingers will move on your instrument, and felt the energy in the room when you step on stage.

All these exercises can help you prepare by compelling you to consider what the upcoming experience will be like. In a similar manner, the Scripture engagement practice that you will learn about this week utilizes the same visualization process. You will be encouraged to place yourself into the biblical story itself and use our senses to experience new and unique perspectives. The main purpose is to not just read the story, but to imagine it more deeply and vividly, as if you were in the scene itself, and thus encountering God in the process.

SHARE

To get things started for this week, discuss the following questions:

- If you participated in the between-session practices the past week, what did you glean from the journaling process? Do you think you would engage in the journaling practice again? If so, how?

- Has there been a time where visualizing a particular situation helped you gain a new perspective or deepen your understanding of something?

WATCH

Watch the video segment for session five. (Play the DVD or see the instructions on the inside front cover on how to access the sessions through streaming). As you watch, use the following outline to record any thoughts or concepts that stand out to you.

The Picture It practice is a natural and simple process. It's one that children tend to do with every story that they hear. They put themselves into the story and experience it as they are listening to it.

Stories are powerful. It's been 2,000 years, and we're still picturing Jesus' stories and being influenced by them. The Bible is God telling us his story. He is revealing himself to us so that we can encounter him and know him. The Bible is the revelation of God. It's how we meet him.

Scripture tells us a bigger story than what our culture tells us. Whose story are we going to believe? Are we going to believe the story we've invented about ourselves, or the cultural story we've been told, or will we believe the story of the Bible? Will we believe that story more than any other that's out there?

We come to the Bible and learn who God is, who we are, and what God says is good and beautiful. These stories invite us to participate in them by engaging our imagination. We find ourselves in the stories, connecting with our emotions and our thoughts. Stories call us to action.

The Picture It practice can be helpful for experiencing God's story in the Bible in a whole-person way. It's especially helpful for those who tend to connect with Scripture on a purely cognitive level. This engagement approach involves our emotions, enveloping our whole person in the process.

We want to approach the Bible so that it's Jesus telling us who we are . . . and we believe it. What we read is not just an idea but reaches into our souls, and then we love out of that truth.

DISCUSS

As you consider what you just watched, use the following questions to discuss these ideas, their basis in Scripture, and their application in your life with your group members.

1. What are some of the ways you have seen children naturally employ the Picture It process? What recollections do you have from your childhood about putting yourself into a story and taking on the role of one of its characters?

2. Read aloud Luke 10:25-37. What approach did Jesus take in answering the man's two questions? Why do you think he took this approach?

3. Read aloud Luke 18:9-14. Why did Jesus tell this particular story? What kind of attitude among the religious leaders was he seeking to address?

4. Review the story of Jesus calming the storm in Matthew 8:23-27 that was used an as example in this week's teaching. Did you see, feel, or imagine anything in this passage that you hadn't before? If so, what was it?

5. How did the Picture It process help you to better relate to what the disciples in the boat were feeling? How do you think you would have reacted in this situation?

6. What did you learn about Jesus through this story? How might Jesus' instructions to have faith in him and not fear apply to a situation that you are facing today?

RESPOND

Take a moment to briefly review the notes you took from the teaching. If you were to take what you experienced and move out in obedience, what would that look like for you?

If you were to try to engage in the Picture It practice *on your own* this week, what would your next steps need to be? Be as specific and practical as possible.

If you were to try to engage in the Picture It practice *with another person* this week, what would your next steps need to be? Again, be as specific and practical as possible.

Picture It Practice Tips:

- Read the text slowly to understand what is happening in the story. Picture the author speaking directly to you and try to imagine the tone of voice he is using. See yourself as one of the characters in the text.
- "Look" around the scene. Where are you? What is happening around you? What does the place feel, sound, look, smell like? Try to really imagine it.
- Dialogue with the characters. What are those around you saying to each other and to you? What do you say to them? What is your discussion like?
- Ask yourself what you're feeling as you interact with the text in this way. Are you happy? Joyful? Full of sorrow? Peaceful? Confused? Full of love? Scared?
- Turn the experience into a prayer and commit to obey what you've learned.

PRAY

As you conclude, close your eyes and remain as still as physically possible. Take a few unrushed moments to envision yourself sitting in the presence of Jesus. What do you see? What do you feel? Do you sense Jesus wanting to say anything to you in this moment? What do you want to say to him? Sit in that silence for a few moments. End by thanking Jesus for his presence and his reassurance that he will always be watching over you when you encounter the storms of life.

Personal Practices

Now that you've explored the Picture It practice of Scripture engagement with your group members, it's time to act on what you've learned. This week, you will be given five daily exercises to help you engage in this Scripture practice and apply what you have learned. When everyone gathers together again next week, there will be time for you to share briefly what you learned or experienced during this personal time of interaction with God's Word.

As you learned in the video teaching for this week, this Scripture engagement practice will help you to get "in the scene" of the story itself so that you can better understand and experience the passage in full effect as robustly as possible. This may be a new or different experience for you, but the challenge this week is to really lean into the experience. Note that you may find it easier to engage with this practice by yourself than with a group.

DAY ONE

Picture the story taking place in Genesis 32:22-32.

Read Genesis 32:22-32. (If the environment lends itself to it, read this story and the other stories that you will be covering this week aloud.) Imagine sitting on a rock near the Jabbock River watching Jacob wrestle with the angel of God—*all night long.* Imagine how exhausted Jacob must have been! What might that wrestling match have been like? Is Jacob dripping with sweat? Is he breathing heavily? Or has he collapsed on the ground in utter fatigue?

What might the voice of the angel have sounded like as he spoke to Jacob?

Picture It

What is the look on Jacob's face when he learned that God has changed his name to Israel? How do you think that made him feel?

What was it like for Jacob when the angel touched his hip so that it was wrenched? Did he wail in pain? What is the look on his face at this turn of events?

What does Jacob's gait look like as he limps? Is it painful to watch him walk?

DAY TWO

Picture the story taking place in John 2:1-11.

Read John 2:1-11. Imagine yourself in this story by using your five senses. First, scan what is happening at the wedding. What are people wearing? What are they doing? What are the expressions on their faces? Are the people dancing, eating, talking, praying?

Is there singing and dancing? Is the music loud or soft? Are the people talking? What are they talking about? What do the wedding songs sound like? Is there laughter at the wedding? Are children laughing or playing games? What does that sound like?

Picture It

What does the food smell like? Is there an aroma of grilled meat, fresh fruit, or just-baked bread? In the hot and dusty setting in first-century Palestine, what do the people smell like?

What does the first batch of wine taste like? How about the second (better) batch of wine? What did the water taste like? How is the meal? Do you want to go back for seconds?

When you greet people at the wedding, what is their embrace like? What is it like to sit on a bench at the banquet? What might it be like for the servants to carry the jars of water? Are they rough or smooth? Are they unbearably heavy?

Now that you've experienced this scene, what would you want to say to God in response? Speak it to him honestly.

DAY THREE

Picture the story taking place in Mark 2:1-12.

Read Mark 2:1-12. Imagine yourself in the room when this happened. What might you be feeling in the midst of all of this—excitement, wonder, confusion, amazement?

Imagine the roof is being opened up above you. Maybe even some of those clumps of dirt are falling on your head. What would that be like for you in that setting? What would you be thinking, feeling, and doing in that moment?

Picture It

Look around the scene. What reactions do you witness in other people? Among Jesus' disciples? What is the look on Jesus' face as he speaks? Can you get a glimpse of the four friends still up on the roof? What are their facial expressions?

What discussion is taking place among the religious leaders as the man is being lowered? What is the look on their faces when Jesus says the man's sins are forgiven? What is their reaction when they discover that Jesus knew what they were thinking in their hearts?

What is the look on the man's face when Jesus tells him to pick up his mat and walk? What excitement do you detect in his voice after the miracle?

Who do you relate to the most in the story: the four friends, the paralytic, the religious leaders, the disciples, or the crowd? Why them?

How has this deepened your understanding of Jesus and those who interacted with him?

DAY FOUR

Picture the story taking place in Mark 3:1-6.

Read Mark 3:1-6. Picture yourself in the synagogue watching the scene play out. What might you be feeling in the midst of all of this—fear, excitement, wonder, shock, amazement, anger?

Picture It

Imagine seeing the man's withered hand grow to be restored again. What would be your first reaction? What would you want to say, ask, or do in that moment if you were the man?

Look around the synagogue. What do you see? What are the other worshipers doing? What is Jesus doing? What is the look on his face? What is the look on the faces of the Pharisees?

Who do you relate to the most in the story? Why that person?

How could this deepen your understanding of Jesus and those who interacted with him?

Imagine walking home from the synagogue that afternoon and bumping into the man whose hand had been restored. What would you say, ask, or do?

Now imagine walking home and bumping into Jesus. What would you want to say to him?

DAY FIVE

Picture the story taking place in Acts 19:21–41.

Imagine that you have accompanied the apostle Paul on his missionary journey to the huge, cosmopolitan, pagan city of Ephesus. You have been sharing the gospel with him there for some time when a riot suddenly breaks out. Read Acts 19:23–41. You and Paul have now been led to the huge amphitheater in Ephesus, which is filled with thousands of angry, riotous residents wanting your heads. Imagine yourself next to your friend.

For two hours, you both hear above you the deafening voices shouting in unison, "Great is Artemis of the Ephesians!" Imagine feeling the walls rumble and move by the power of their unified voices. Despite the clear and present danger, your friend still wants to tell the angry crowd of the good news of Jesus' death and resurrection. You try to convince him this would not be wise, but he still wants to go. What are you feeling in this moment?

What emotions are you feeling about your friend Paul?

What words are you using to try to persuade him to refrain from walking out onto the theater floor? What other attempts or arguments might you be trying to use to deter his efforts?

The city secretary has now quieted the angry mob and dispersed the crowd. How are you, your friends, and Paul processing the event?

What are you feeling now that calm has been restored?

Picture It

Based on your perspective of being in the Ephesian theater, how does that shape your prayers today? What do you sense the Lord wants to give you from this in-the-scene experience?

CONTEMPLATE

"Be strong and very courageous. Be careful to obey all the law my servant Moses gave you; do not turn from it to the right or to the left, that you may be successful wherever you go. Keep this Book of the Law always on your lips; meditate on it day and night, so that you may be careful to do everything written in it. Then you will be prosperous and successful."

JOSHUA 1:7-8

WELCOME

Perhaps you've driven down the road lately and been met with the flashing yellow lights that indicate you've just entered a "school zone." State governments and school districts want to ensure safety for students, teachers, and parents during school days, so they significantly reduce the speed limits in these zones. Many states post limits of twenty-five miles per hour—some as low as fifteen miles per hour—and mandate hefty fines for violators.

Certainly, it is good and right that states post these limits. But on a personal level, many of us know just how difficult it is to *actually* slow down while travelling through these zones, especially when we are running late or in a hurry. At times, it feels like the car is moving so slowly that it might be faster to get out and run instead. Yet, difficult as it may be, slowing down not only keeps the areas around the schools safe, but it also helps us see new details we may not have noticed before—like all the little pedestrians wearing backpacks.

In much the same way, when we speed read Scripture, we miss out on noticing important details in the passage. We are often in a rush to get on with our day, or we want to be as efficient as possible in our Bible reading. But slowing down—difficult as it may be—helps us to notice new details, ponder the current condition of our souls, and truly listen for what God is saying to us through the text and what new insights he is providing.

In this final Scripture engagement practice, it will be important for you to slow down and envision yourself moving through a school zone. It may be difficult (especially if you are a driven person who possesses a Type-A personality), but it is for the benefit of others—and for your own soul. As one theologian said, "The speed of godliness is slow." God seems to show up most often when we slow down and pay attention in the present moment.

SHARE

To get things started this final week, discuss the following questions:

- How would you rate your ability to slow down at times to just hear what God might be saying to you? How naturally does this come to you?

- Which of the Scripture engagement practices has been most enlightening for you? Why do you think that particular one was the most significant for you?

WATCH

Watch the video segment for session six. (Play the DVD or see the instructions on the inside front cover on how to access the sessions through streaming). As you watch, use the following outline to record any thoughts or concepts that stand out to you.

The Contemplate engagement practice has been around for hundreds of years. The church fathers referred to as *lectio divina*, which means "divine reading" or "holy reading." If you've read the Bible for any amount of time, you've probably participated in the contemplate process before.

There are four steps in the process: (1) read, (2) meditate, (3) pray, and (4) contemplate. It is a bit like learning to play the piano. You need to learn where to put your fingers and where to press down on certain keys. It can feel disjointed at first, but over time it starts to flow.

The Contemplate practice is also like "eating" Scripture. *Reading* is taking a bite of food. *Meditating* is chewing on it. *Praying* is savoring it. *Contemplate* is digesting the food and making it a part of your body. The practice helps you to slow down, savor your time in God's Word, and find joy in meeting God.

Contemplate

Anytime you engage with Scripture, the more you understand the passage and have read through it, the more it will enhance your time with God. You need at least a basic understanding of the passage. When you go through the Contemplate process, you don't want to be making up things about the Bible.

Something amazing happens as we bring the Bible and our lives together. Scripture, meditation, and prayer are the heart of what it means to engage the Bible so we will grow in our relationship with God.

People often say that at the end of a contemplate session, they have a feeling of closeness and intimacy with the Lord. One of the most valuable things we can do with this feeling is to embrace it and just be with God. We don't need to always be *talking at* God. It's really powerful to just be quiet.

DISCUSS

As you consider what you just watched, use the following questions to discuss these ideas, their basis in Scripture, and their application in your life with your group members.

1. In this week's teaching, it was mentioned that contemplating Scripture is like eating a great meal. Think of the last time you enjoyed a really good meal. Who was there? What was the occasion? What was served? What made it so great?

2. Some of us read Scripture like we're hitting the drive-thru at a fast-food restaurant. Can you think of a time where you sat down to an enjoyable "meal" of feasting on God's Word? What was it like? How was it different from other times you spent in Scripture?

3. *Read* aloud Psalm 1:1–3, which was the example used for the Contemplate process during this week's teaching. Is there something in the passage that connects with you at a deeper level—perhaps a single word, phrase, sentence, or image that catches your eye and connects with you emotionally in a special way?

4. Take a moment as a group to *meditate* on those words, phrases, or images that stood out to you. Why do you think those resonate with you? What might the Holy Spirit be saying about you or another person in your life through those words and images?

5. Now consider how the Holy Spirit might be leading you to *pray.* What do you want to say to God in this moment after reflecting on this passage?

6. The fourth stage of the Contemplate practice is also called *contemplate.* The task in this stage is to simply be silent in the presence of the Lord. How easy or difficult is this for you? What distractions tend to get in the way of you just being in God's presence?

RESPOND

Take a moment to briefly review the notes you took from the teaching. What do you believe was the most important element for you to take with you in the weeks ahead?

Invite someone to read the following paragraphs aloud to the group:

> *Hundreds of years ago, the Christian communities would have a book or tablet where everyone would write down what they heard from the Lord after contemplating Scripture together. Even though they had read and prayed the same passage together, they rejoiced in the fact that the Lord had given each one of them a different word or phrase from the passage. This exercise of writing down what had been given to them was called florilegium, which in Latin means "to pick the flowers." In a sense, they would all bring their individual "flowers" and share it with the community, thus creating a beautiful arrangement.*

Take a few moments now to *contemplate* what you have read in Psalm 1:1–3. Spend two to three minutes in silence sitting in the presence of God, listening for any ways that he might be guiding you to act on what you've read. At the end of the time, write your thoughts below. Then take a few minutes to share some of these "flowers" with the rest of the group.

Contemplate Practice Tips:

- Choose a place and time that is quiet and uninterrupted. You will need at least fifteen minutes to get the most out of this practice.

- Consider which passage to use, whether a lengthy passage or only a few verses. A smaller portion of Scripture will give you a more in-depth idea of the passage, which is what Contemplate is all about. But a longer passage can give you a more general understanding of Scripture as a whole. (Note that if you are just starting out with this practice, it is best to use a shorter passage.)

- Contemplate is not meant to introduce you to something new in the Bible but for you to "feed" on what you know. There are an infinite number of ways to choose daily Scripture readings, so be creative and use your resources! If you are stuck and really don't know what passage to read, start with Psalm 23.

- Before you start reading, ask the Holy Spirit to quiet your mind and bless your time in Scripture. Remind yourself that you are coming to God's Word and that to engage with the Bible is to engage with God!
- If you get distracted or tired, don't criticize yourself. Simply bring your mind back to the Bible passage, re-read it, and be grateful for God's Word.

PRAY

End this study by having everyone open his or her hands in a posture of receiving from God. Ask if one or two people would offer a prayer of thanksgiving to God for how his Word has spoken to them—and how his Word still speaks to all of us today. Then ask God to give you the grace and faith to live out what has been entrusted to you in obedience in the weeks ahead.

SESSION SIX

Personal Practices

N ow that you've explored the final Contemplate practice with your group members, it's time to act on what
you've learned. This week, you will be given five daily exercises to help you engage in this Scripture practice and apply
what you have learned. In this final time of reflection, you
may also want to review the other practices, either going
back to previous personal studies in this guide or referring
to the journal or notebook you used for your responses. In
the coming days, be sure to share any insights you learned
with one of your fellow group members.

As stated during the group session time, the Contemplate
practice has been around for hundreds of years. In the early
church this was known as *Lectio divina,* which in Latin
means "divine reading" or "holy reading." One ancient leader
compared the four steps in the process to rungs on a ladder,
using four additional Latin words: *lectio* (reading), *meditatio*
(meditation), *oratio* (prayer), and *contemplatio* (contemplate).
Utilizing each rung of the ladder during this week will help
you climb higher up to a deeper connection with God!

DAY ONE

Contemplate the words of Psalm 100:1–5.

Read the words of Psalm 100 printed below. Then read the psalm again, but slightly slower. Read it a third time, this time even slower than before.

> Shout for joy to the LORD, all the earth.
>> Worship the LORD with gladness;
>> come before him with joyful songs.
> Know that the LORD is God.
>> It is he who made us, and we are his;
>> we are his people, the sheep of his pasture.
>
> Enter his gates with thanksgiving
>> and his courts with praise;
>> give thanks to him and praise his name.
> For the LORD is good and his love endures forever;
>> his faithfulness continues through all generations.

Now *meditate* on what you read. Is there any word, phrase, or sentence that sticks out to you? Is there anything that felt like your mind took a highlighter to a portion of the text? What is that phrase or word? Write it down in the space below.

Contemplate

Next, *pray*. Sit with that word, phrase, or sentence for a moment. In quiet reflection, ask God, "Lord, why did you give me this word or phrase?" Just listen for his response. Then record below what you sensed the Lord gave to you.

Finally, *contemplate*. Focus on simply being with the Lord. After a moment, ask, "Lord, how might you want me to steward what you've given to me in this time? Write down any directions that you feel the Holy Spirit is providing to you in the space below.

DAY TWO

Contemplate the words of Isaiah 40:26-31.

Set a timer for six minutes, and then *read* the words in Isaiah 40:26-31 (either silently or out loud) printed below. When you finish the passage, start over again and reread it. Continue to read the passage repeatedly until the timer rings. (Don't rush the process on this—just slow down and savor each verse in this passage. Let it wash over you as you read).

Lift up your eyes and look to the heavens:
    Who created all these?
He who brings out the starry host one by one
    and calls forth each of them by name.
Because of his great power and mighty strength,
    not one of them is missing.

Why do you complain, Jacob?
    Why do you say, Israel,
*"My way is hidden from the L*ORD*;*
    my cause is disregarded by my God"?
Do you not know?
    Have you not heard?
*The L*ORD *is the everlasting God,*
    the Creator of the ends of the earth.
He will not grow tired or weary,
    and his understanding no one can fathom.
He gives strength to the weary
    and increases the power of the weak.
Even youths grow tired and weary,

Contemplate

and young men stumble and fall;
but those who hope in the LORD
*   will renew their strength.*
They will soar on wings like eagles;
*   they will run and not grow weary,*
*   they will walk and not be faint.*

Now *meditate* on what you read. Is there a word or phrase that remains in your mind or heart? Say that word or phrase aloud, and then record it in the space below.

Next, *pray.* Ask the Lord, "Is there anything you'd like me to know or be reminded of with this word or phrase as it relates to my life?" Record any responses in the space below.

Finally, *contemplate*. Based on what you received from God in this time, this may lead to a time of praise for who he is or a time of confession and repentance. It may prompt you to petition God for a specific request, or it may lead you to intercede on behalf of a family member, friend, neighbor, coworker, or colleague. Let your prayers guide you during this time. Write down any directions you feel the Lord is asking you to take in the space below.

DAY THREE

Contemplate the words of Romans 11:33–36.
Read the following words from Paul about the greatness of God from Romans 11:33–36. Then read the words again at a slightly slower pace than you did the first time. Finally, read the passage a third time at an even slower pace, focusing on each word as you read it.

> Oh, the depth of the riches of the wisdom and knowledge
> of God!
> How unsearchable his judgments,
> and his paths beyond tracing out!
> "Who has known the mind of the Lord?
> Or who has been his counselor?"

Contemplate

"Who has ever given to God,
that God should repay them?"
For from him and through him and for him are all things.
To him be the glory forever! Amen.

Now *meditate* on what you read. Locate one word or phrase that rises to the surface of your mind and heart. Write it down.

What does this word or phrase tell you about the nature or character of God?

How have you experienced or encountered that element of God's nature or character?

Next, *pray.* Thank God for that aspect of his character. Ponder the supremacy of God and how he is unlike anyone or anything else in the entire universe. Let these ponderings lead you to a time of thanking him for who he is. Record below any specific praises that come to mind.

Finally, *contemplate.* How can that word, phrase, or element of God's character shape how you move out into the world today? How could it impact your life right now—your level of joy, the peace you feel in life, and your ability to live with deeper humility or gratitude?

DAY FOUR

Contemplate the words of Ephesians 2:4-10.

Read the following words from Paul about God's great love for us from Ephesians 2:4-10. Since this might be a familiar passage to you, the passages printed below are from the *New Living* and *The Message* translations of the Bible. When you are finished, read the passage again in one of the translations, pausing for a moment between each verse.

> *But God is so rich in mercy, and he loved us so much, that even though we were dead because of our sins, he gave us life when he raised Christ from the dead. (It is only by God's grace that you have been saved!) For he raised us from the dead along with Christ and seated us with him in the heavenly realms because we are united with Christ Jesus. So God can point to us in all future ages as examples of the incredible wealth of his grace and kindness toward us, as shown in all he has done for us who are united with Christ Jesus.*
>
> *God saved you by his grace when you believed. And you can't take credit for this; it is a gift from God. Salvation is not a reward for the good things we have done, so none of us can boast about it. For we are God's masterpiece. He has created us anew in Christ Jesus, so we can do the good things he planned for us long ago (NLT).*
>
> *It's a wonder God didn't lose his temper and do away with the whole lot of us. Instead, immense in mercy and with an incredible love, he embraced us. He took our sin-dead lives and made us alive in Christ. He did all this on his own, with no*

help from us! Then he picked us up and set us down in highest heaven in company with Jesus, our Messiah.

Now God has us where he wants us, with all the time in this world and the next to shower grace and kindness upon us in Christ Jesus. Saving is all his idea, and all his work. All we do is trust him enough to let him do it. It's God's gift from start to finish! We don't play the major role. If we did, we'd probably go around bragging that we'd done the whole thing! No, we neither make nor save ourselves. God does both the making and saving. He creates each of us by Christ Jesus to join him in the work he does, the good work he has gotten ready for us to do, work we had better be doing (MSG).

Now *meditate* on what you read. What remains with you? What one word, concept, phrase, or verse "lifts up off the page" in your mind? What stays with you?

Next, *pray.* Consider your life—the fears, joys, hopes, and current situations and opportunities that you are facing. How might those dynamics be impacted by what you sense the Holy Spirit has given to you as you read and reread the Scripture?

Contemplate

Finally, *contemplate*. As you read Paul's words to the Ephesian church, how might they apply to you today in your context? What would faithful obedience look like for you if you were to live out this particular word, phrase, or passage in your life this week? Write it below.

DAY FIVE

Contemplate the words of Titus 3:3-7.

Read the following words from Paul about the kindness and goodness of God from Titus 3:3-7, noticing the presence of the Triune God (Father, Son, and Holy Spirit) in this passage. Read it a second time, pausing for a moment at the end of each verse before beginning again. On your third reading, emphasize the pronouns listed in bold in the passage.

> *At one time **we** too were foolish, disobedient, deceived and enslaved by all kinds of passions and pleasures. **We** lived in malice and envy, being hated and hating one another. But when the kindness and love of God **our** Savior appeared, he saved **us**, not because of righteous things **we** had done, but because of his mercy. He saved **us** through the washing of rebirth and renewal by the Holy Spirit, whom he poured out on **us** generously through Jesus Christ **our** Savior, so that, having been justified by his grace, **we** might become heirs having the hope of eternal life.*

Now *meditate* on what you read. Take note of what jumped out at you and write the word or phrase below.

Next, *pray.* Ask, "Lord, why did you give me this word or phrase?" Sit in silence. Listen. Ponder. Wait. Listen some more. After a few moments, consider whether the passage is for you personally or something the Lord wants you to do, say, serve, give, or bless someone else with. Record your thoughts on this in the space below.

Finally, *contemplate.* How could you live in faithful response and obedience to God today based on what he revealed to you?

NOW WHAT?

Often at the end of a group study, it's common to ask, "Now what?" Even though the official group study time is finished, it doesn't mean you have to stop engaging with Scripture! Here are four practical and specific next steps you can take to move forward.

Step #1: Review the notes from this study.

Reviewing what the group covered is an important way to reinforce what you've learned and be reminded of what you've all experienced. Take ten minutes and thumb through the pages in this study. Review the lesson notes. Notice what you wrote down. Be reminded of the questions in each section. Remember what you and the others shared during the past several weeks. Think through each of the engagement exercises the group participated in together:

- Praying Scripture

- Engaging with Art

- Journaling Scripture

- Picturing Scripture

- Contemplating Scripture

Use the reflection questions below to guide your time of review. Consider recording your reflections and responses below

Which engagement practice surprised you the most? Why?

Which engagement practice was most difficult for you? Why that one?

Through which practice did you connect with God most deeply?

What passage of Scripture remains with you the most? How does that passage give you a clearer picture of who God is and/or how he works in the hearts of people?

What is the most important reminder, encouragement, or "aha" moment the Lord gave you through this study?

How will you faithfully steward what God has given to you?

How will this study impact the way you think about and/or approach Scripture?

Step #2: *Pause and thank God for how he revealed himself to you.*

Turn off your phone, put away your screens, and sit for a moment in silence. After a few moments, thank the Lord for how he has used his Word in your life and the lives of those in your group to speak to you. If helpful, use the following prompts.

Father, thank you for revealing yourself to me in this journey through . . .

Jesus, I am grateful to you for showing me more of who you are through ...

Holy Spirit, thank you for reminding me of _____ in the verse/ passage that I read in _____.

Step #3: Continue to participate in these Scripture engagement practices.

Choose one or two of the practices you participated in that most connected with your "heart language." Make a commitment to engage in them twice a week for the next four weeks. Write down the practices that you want to commit to continuing to engage with.

Practice 1:

Practice 2:

Step #4: Consider picking up a copy of The Abide Bible.

The Abide Bible was created by thirty-three different writers who created 2,500 Scripture engagement prompts using the five practices that you've learned throughout this study. Several prompts are found throughout all sixty-six books of the Bible. Note that *The Abide Bible* is not a Study Bible—at least not in the traditional sense of the word. Instead, it is a participation-oriented Bible designed to help you deepen your relationship with Christ through the journey of Scripture engagement. In other words, it will help you continue to do exactly what you've been doing. You can engage with these prompts and practices individually or with a group. (For additional information about *The Abide Bible,* see the back of this study guide.)

A final word of encouragement to leave with you: *keep going.* You've had a wonderful start to the journey of Scripture engagement. Don't stop now. As the author of Hebrews wrote, "The word of God is alive and active. Sharper than any double-edged sword, it penetrates even to dividing soul and spirit, joints and marrow" (4:12). The Word of God is *alive* and *active.* This means that—in spite of being written thousands of years ago—it still has the power to teach, remind, guide, encourage, and challenge you today.

So keep going! Don't just read the Bible . . . but seek to continually *engage* with Scripture. In doing so, God will meet you and abide with you in the process.

ADDITIONAL RESOURCES

The Abide Bible

To learn more about *The Abide Bible*, watch testimonials, read endorsements, and to download digital samples, check out www.thomasnelsonbibles.com/abide-bible.

Scripture Engagement Context and Resources

For additional context and information about Scripture engagement, as well as additional articles about Scripture engagement, visit www.thomasnelsonbibles.com/abide-bible /about-scripture-engagement.

Bible Gateway Scripture Engagement Resources

Biblegateway.com is a free website designed to help people read and study God's Word. It contains more than 230 different translations and versions of the Bible in more than seventy languages. The website has an entire section on Scripture Engagement practices that you can utilize to further your own engagement journey. For more information, visit https:// www.biblegateway.com/resources/scripture-engagement.

The Center for Scripture Engagement

Dr. Phil Collins serves as co-executive chair of the Center for Scripture Engagement and Professor of Christian Ministries at Taylor University in Upland, Indiana. You can learn more by visiting https://www.taylor.edu/center-for-scripture-engagement.

Christian Life Survey

This free survey takes approximately fifteen to twenty minutes to complete and will help you clarify the center points of your spiritual life, identify your preferred ways of engaging spiritually, and will suggest practical and creative ways to engage with Scripture based on your results. Beyond your individual results you can also use an option to take the survey as a group and get the overall results for your group. To access the survey, go to taylor.edu/christianlifesurvey.

LEADER'S GUIDE

Thank you for your willingness to lead a small group through this study. What you have chosen to do is valuable and will make a great difference in the lives of others. The rewards of being a leader are different from those of participating, and we hope that as you lead you will find your own walk with Jesus deepened by the experience.

The Abide Bible Course is a six-session Bible study built around video content and small-group interaction. As the group leader, imagine yourself as the host of a party. Your job is to take care of your guests by managing the behind-the-scenes details so that as your guests arrive, they can focus on one another and on the interaction around the topic for that week.

Your role as the group leader is not to answer all the questions or reteach the content—the video, book, and study guide will do most of that work. Your job is to guide the experience and cultivate your small group into a connected and engaged community. This will make it a place for members to process, question, and reflect—not necessarily receive more instruction.

There are several elements in this leader's guide that will help you as you structure your study and reflection time, so be sure to follow along and take advantage of each one.

Before You Begin

Before your first meeting, make sure the group members have a copy of this study guide. Alternately, you can hand out the study guides at your first meeting and give the members some time to look over the material and ask any preliminary questions. Also make sure they are aware that they have access to the videos at any time through the streaming code provided on the inside front cover. During your first meeting, send a sheet of paper around the room and have the members write down their name, phone number, and email address so you can keep in touch with them during the week.

Generally, the ideal size for a group is eight to ten people, which will ensure that everyone has enough time to participate in discussions. If you have more people, you might want to break up the main group into smaller subgroups. Encourage those who show up at the first meeting to commit to attending the duration of the study, as this will help the group members get to know one another, create stability for the group, and help you know how to best prepare each week.

Each of the sessions begins with an opening reflection. The questions that follow in the "Share" section serve as an icebreaker to get the group members thinking about the general topic at hand. Some people may want to tell a long story in response to one of these questions, but the goal is to keep the answers brief. Ideally, you want everyone in the group to get a chance to answer, so try to keep the responses to a minute or less. If you have talkative group members, say up front that everyone needs to limit their answer to one minute.

Give the group members a chance to answer, but also tell them to feel free to pass if they wish. With the rest of the study, it's generally not a good idea to have everyone answer every question—a free-flowing discussion is more desirable. But with the opening icebreaker-type questions, you can go around the circle. Encourage shy people to share, but don't force them.

At your first meeting, let the group members know each session contains a personal study section that they can use to engage in each of the Scripture engagement practices on their own during the week. These exercises will help the members cement the concepts presented during the group study time and encourage them to spend time each day in God's Word. Let them know that if they choose to do so, they can watch the video for the following week by accessing the streaming code found on the inside front cover of their studies. Invite them to bring any questions and insights they uncovered while reading to your next meeting, especially if they had a breakthrough moment or didn't understand something.

Weekly Preparation

As the leader, there are a few things you should do to prepare for each meeting:

- *Read through the session.* This will help you to become more familiar with the content and know how to structure the discussion times.

- *Decide how the videos will be used.* Determine whether you want the members to watch the videos ahead of time (via the streaming access code found on the inside front cover) or together as a group.

- *Decide which questions you want to discuss.* Based on the amount and length of group discussion, you may not be able to get through all the questions, so choose four to five that you definitely want to cover.

- *Be familiar with the questions you want to discuss.* When the group meets, you'll be watching the clock, so you want to make sure you are familiar with the questions you have selected. In this way, you'll ensure you have the material more deeply in your mind than your group members.

- *Pray for your group.* Pray for your group members throughout the week and ask God to lead them as they study his Word.

In many cases, there will be no one "right" answer to the question. Answers will vary, especially when the group members are being asked to share their personal experiences.

Structuring the Discussion Time

You will need to determine with your group how long you want to meet each week so you can plan your time accordingly. Generally, most groups like to meet for either ninety minutes or two hours, so you could use one of the following schedules:

Leader's Guide

SECTION	90 MINUTES	120 MINUTES
Welcome (members arrive and get settled)	10 minutes	15 minutes
Share (discuss one or more of the opening questions for the session)	15 minutes	20 minutes
Watch (watch the teaching material together and take notes)	20 minutes	20 minutes
Discuss (discuss the Bible study questions you selected ahead of time)	35 minutes	50 minutes
Respond/Pray (reflect on the video content, pray together as a group, and dismiss)	10 minutes	15 minutes

As the group leader, it is up to you to keep track of the time and keep things on schedule. You might want to set a timer for each segment so both you and the group members know when your time is up. (There are some good phone apps for timers that play a gentle chime or other pleasant sound instead of a disruptive noise.)

Don't be concerned if the group members are quiet or slow to share. People are often quiet when they are pulling together their ideas, and this might be a new experience for them. Just ask a question and let it hang in the air until someone shares. You can then say, "Thank you. What about others? What came to you when you watched that portion of the teaching?"

Group Dynamics

Leading a group through *The Abide Bible Course* will prove to be highly rewarding both to you and your group members. But you still may encounter challenges along the way! Discussions can get off track. Group members may not be sensitive to the needs and ideas of others. Some might worry they will be expected to talk about matters that make them feel awkward. Others may express comments that result in disagreements. To help ease this strain on you and the group, consider the following ground rules:

- When someone raises a question or comment that is off the main topic, suggest that you deal with it another time, or, if you feel led to go in that direction, let the group know you will be spending some time discussing it.

- If someone asks a question that you don't know how to answer, admit it and move on. At your discretion, feel free to invite group members to comment on questions that call for personal experience.

- If you find one or two people are dominating the discussion time, direct a few questions to others in the group. Outside the main group time, ask the more dominating members to help you draw out the quieter ones. Work to make them a part of the solution instead of part of the problem.

- When a disagreement occurs, encourage the group members to process the matter in love. Encourage those on opposite sides to restate what they heard the other side say about the matter, and then invite each side to evaluate if that perception is accurate. Lead the group in examining other Scriptures related to the topic and look for common ground.

When any of these issues arise, encourage your group members to follow these words from the Bible: "Love one another" (John 13:34), "If it is possible, as far as it depends on you, live at peace with everyone" (Romans 12:18), "Whatever is true . . . noble . . . right . . . if anything is excellent or praiseworthy—think about such things" (Philippians 4:8), and "Be quick to listen, slow to speak and slow to become angry" (James 1:19). This will make your group time more rewarding and beneficial for everyone who attends.

Thank you again for taking the time to lead your group. You are making a difference in the lives of others and having an impact on the kingdom of God.

Also Available

The research is clear. A vibrant, transforming relationship with God starts with engaging His Word and reflecting on it. But many don't know how to delve deeper or know what techniques they can use to enrich their time in the Bible beyond reading plans and academic study. The *Abide Bible* and the *Abide Study Journals* both guide and teach Scripture engagement with prompts for five proven methods so that the Word may "dwell in you richly" (Colossians 3:16 NKJV).

Go to AbideBible.com

*Free Scripture engagement method
training and samples*

TAYLOR UNIVERSITY CENTER FOR
**SCRIPTURE
ENGAGEMENT**

BibleGateway

Thomas Nelson
Since 1798